JESUS! HIS DEITY AND POWER REVEALED!

Oliver Rankine

© Copyright – 2025

All Rights Reserved. No part of this book may be reproduced, stored in a retrieval system, or transmitted by any means without the written permission of the author.

Cover Design: BK Royston Publishing

ISBN-13: 978-1-955501-31-6

King James Version Scriptural Text – Public Domain

Printed in the United States of America

Acknowledgements

I give honor to our Creator and Savior, Jesus Christ, for His love and mercy, who has inspired me over the years, with the divine inspiration and knowledge to reveal His Deity and power in this context that others may also receive this revelation as I have.
Thanks to Pastor Leroy Leslie for his support and guidance, on this journey.

TABLE OF CONTENTS

Acknowledgements	**iii**
Introduction	**vii**
Chapter 1 **God with Us**	**1**
Chapter 2 **Who Do Men Say I am?**	**25**
Chapter 3 **His Deity**	**43**
Chapter 4 **The Great Mystery**	**59**
Chapter 5 **I and my Father am one**	**73**
Chapter 6 **God Our Only Savior** **Jesus the only Savior**	**85**
Chapter 7 **God Our Redeemer Jesus our Redeemer**	**91**

Introduction

These words are an inspirational commentary given by the power of the Holy Spirit, through divine guidance and direction, and have been in progress for many years.
The intent of these words is for revelation and knowledge of the deity and power of our redeemer and Creator, Jesus Christ.
There are scriptural references for further edification and clarity.
I hope that, as I have, these words will also open your heart to the knowledge and understanding of our God and Savior, Jesus Christ.
And I believe that as He has revealed Himself to me, He will to everyone who believes!

Chapter 1

God with us

Where do I begin? How do I begin to describe his deity?
Jesus Christ, the ultimate conception of the plan of salvation, has revolutionized the gospel of the kingdom. Generations came, and generations passed; we have heard of great men and prophets of old, mighty men of valor, men of wisdom, power, and might, but none to compare. Jesus was born contrary to the laws of nature; He defied the laws of science and the concepts of Judges and Kings.
His compatibility with humanity has no affiliation as to his majesty, power, and might, yet He spoke these words in Matthew 11: 11 concerning his birth,
 Not to demystify the mystery of his supremacy to humanity but, rather, to reveal the truth of his deity, power, and supremacy.

Matthew 11:11, *"Verily I say unto you, among them that are born of women   there hath not risen a greater than John the Baptist:*

Notwithstanding he that is least in the kingdom of heaven is greater than he."

Yet, we know that both Jesus and John were born of a woman. We also know that John, in all his powers, cannot be compared with the majesty and power of the Lord Jesus Christ. John himself admits Jesus' superiority in Mark, Chapter 1. While he baptized Jesus in the river Jordan, John admitted that Jesus is mightier than he. God ordained John the Baptist as the forerunner, a messenger sent before Jesus to prepare the way of the Lord. John was the messenger crying in the wilderness, "Prepare ye the way of the Lord." Prophesied by Isaiah the Prophet;

Isaiah:40:3.
The voice of him that crieth in the wilderness, Prepare ye the way of the Lord, make straight in the desert a highway for our God.

Mark 1:2-10, *"As it is written in the prophets, Behold, I send my messenger before thy face, which shall prepare thy way before thee.*

3 The voice of one crying in the wilderness, Prepare ye the way of the Lord, make his paths straight.

4 John was baptized in the wilderness and preached the baptism of repentance for the remission of sins.

5 And there went out unto him all the land of Judaea, and they of Jerusalem, and were all baptized of him in the river of Jordan, confessing their sins.

7 And preached, saying. There cometh one mightier than I after me, the latchet of whose shoes I am not worthy to stoop down and unloose.

8 I indeed have baptized you with water: but he shall baptize you with the Holy Ghost.

9 And it came to pass in those days, that Jesus came from Nazareth of Galilee, and was baptized of John in Jordan.

10 And straightway coming up out of the water, he saw the heavens opened, and the Spirit like a dove descending upon him:

John 1:32-33, *"And John bare record, saying, I saw the Spirit descending from heaven like a dove, and it abode upon him.*

And I knew him not: but he that sent me to baptize with water, the same said unto me, upon whom thou shalt see the Spirit descending, and remaining on him, the same is he which baptizes with the Holy Spirit."

John esteemed Jesus highly; he admits he was not worthy even to unlatch Jesus' shoes. He was humble enough to acknowledge that he was not the light but came to bear witness of the only true light, Jesus Christ! That would light up this world. So, was Jesus placing a distinction between his birth and John's?
Was Jesus' birth so much different from that of John the Baptist?
Amazingly! There are some interesting similarities related to the births of Jesus and John the Baptist. They were both born of a woman and have similar birth events.

Their births were both contrary to the laws of nature.
The scriptures indicate the natural conditions of the two women. Mary and Elizabeth both thought they couldn't conceive a child. One was a virgin, and the other was too old to conceive a child.

Jesus was born of a virgin. **Luke 1:26-35,** *"And in the sixth month the angel Gabriel was sent from God unto a city of Galilee, named Nazareth,*

27 To a virgin espoused to a man whose name was Joseph, of the house of David; and the virgin's name was Mary.

28 And the angel came in unto her, and said, Hail, thou that art highly favored, the Lord is with thee: blessed art thou among women.

29 And when she saw him, she was troubled at his saying, and cast in her mind what manner of salutation this should be.

30 And the angel said unto her, Fear not, Mary: for thou hast found favor with God.

31 And, behold, thou shalt conceive in thy womb, and bring forth a son, and shalt call his name JESUS.

32 He shall be great, and shall be called the Son of the Highest: and the Lord God shall give unto him the throne of his father David:

33 And he shall reign over the house of Jacob forever; and of his kingdom there shall be no end.

34 Then said Mary unto the angel, How shall this be, seeing I know not a man?

35 And the angel answered and said unto her, The Holy Ghost shall come upon thee, and the power of the Highest shall overshadow thee: therefore, also that holy thing which shall be born of thee shall be called the Son of God."

Mary was described by the angel as blessed among women and well favored by God a wonderful position to be in.
However, Mary could neither perceive nor fathom the wonders of God's power that would manifest through her.

Both births and names were prophesied by the same angel, Gabriel, a messenger from God.

Jesus – Matthew 1:20-21, *"But while he thought on these things, behold, the angel of the Lord appeared unto him in a dream, saying, Joseph, thou son of David, fear not to take unto thee Mary thy wife: for that which is conceived in her is of the Holy Ghost. And she shall bring forth a son, and* thou shalt call his name JESUS: for he shall save his people from their sins.

John – Luke 1:5-13, "There was in the days of Herod, the king of Judaea, a certain priest named Zacharias, of the course of Abia: and his wife was of the daughters of Aaron, and her name was Elisabeth.

6 And they were both righteous before God, walking in all the commandments and ordinances of the Lord blameless.

7 And they had no child because Elisabeth was barren, and they both were now well stricken in years.

8 And it came to pass that while he executed the priest's office before God in the order of his course,

9 According to the custom of the priest's office, his lot was to burn incense when he went into the temple of the Lord.

10 And the whole multitude of the people were praying without at the time of incense.

11 And there appeared unto him an angel of the Lord standing on the right side of the altar of incense.

12 And when Zacharias saw him, he was troubled, and fear fell upon him.

13 But the angel said unto him, Fear not, Zacharias: for thy prayer is heard; and thy wife Elisabeth shall bear thee a son, and thou shalt call his name John."

Both were born with the Spirit of the Lord.

John was the first person to receive the Holy Spirit in his mother's womb before his birth.

However, this may have been the most significant reason why Jesus said that among those born of a woman, there is none greater than John, and also, he was called to go before Jesus.

Luke 1:15, *"For he shall be great in the sight of the Lord, and shall drink neither wine nor strong drink; and he shall be filled with the Holy Ghost, even from his mother's womb.*

Jesus said in **Matthew:1:20**, "But while he thought on these things, behold, the angel of the Lord appeared unto him in a dream, saying, Joseph, thou son of David, fear not to take unto thee Mary thy wife: for that which is conceived in her is of the Holy Ghost."

Both would do incredible things.

Luke:1:15-17, "For he shall be great in the sight of the Lord, and shall drink neither wine nor strong drink; and he shall be filled with the Holy Ghost, even from his mother's womb

16: And many of the children of Israel shall he turn to the Lord their God.

17: And he shall go before him in the spirit and power of Elias, to turn the hearts of the fathers to the children, and the disobedient to the wisdom of the just; to make ready a people prepared for the Lord."

In **Matthew 1:21,** "And she shall bring forth a son, and thou shalt call his name JESUS: for he shall save his people from their sins."

So, was Jesus highlighting that, unlike John the Baptist's natural birth, His was spiritual? John evidently was the first man to receive the Holy Spirit, even before his birth. However, this would not uniquely identify him as the most remarkable man since other men have received the Holy Ghost afterward, and the operative words Jesus used were "AMONG THEM THAT ARE BORN OF WOMEN." Or was he indicating that John was of this Earth, earthly, and He was of the Kingdom of God, heavenly? As He continued to say, however, that the least in the kingdom of heaven is more significant than John. Jesus clarifies his statement by saying: "Notwithstanding he that is least in the kingdom of heaven is greater than he (John)."

This confirms that Jesus is of the heavenly kingdom, not earthly. Then, to whom shall I liken him, or where is his place in humanity? It was Isaiah who first prophesied of his birth in

***Isaiah 7:14*. Therefore, the Lord himself shall give you a sign; Behold, a virgin shall conceive and bear a son, and his name shall be called Immanuel,** *meaning God with Us.*

The scripture says the LORD himself, specifying he would reveal the sign, be a partaker of the sign, by stepping out of divinity into humanity, channeled into humanity through the womb of a virgin.

This specific scripture not only emphasizes but fulfilled the sign of Jesus' mysterious entry into humanity; one may wonder why. Did he have to enter the world in this manner?

There are some profound reasons for his mysterious entry, which we will discuss later. However, the main reason is to accomplish the plan of salvation for humanity, redeeming us from sin. And was prophesied by Isaiah the Prophet about 735 BC.

This was fulfilled hundreds of years later, in the book of Matthew, when the angel told Mary that she would bear a son, and His name shall be called "JESUS." However, Isaiah prophesied that **His name shall be called** "IMMANUEL." In **Isaiah 7:14**, was this an error? Did someone make a mistake with his name, or is Jesus simply God with Us, which is the meaning of Immanuel?
In Isaiah's prophecy, the actual name was not revealed; however, his prophecy was to be

fulfilled hundreds of years later, with the exact revelation of his prophecy, meaning the child Jesus is God with us, which is the interpretation of Immanuel.

"For unto us a child is born unto us, a son is given, and the government shall be on his shoulders. **And he Shall be called** *Wonderful, Counselor, the Mighty God, the Everlasting Father, Prince of Peace."*(**Isaiah 9:6**).

In Matthew, Jesus mentioned that He came to fulfill the laws and prophets;

Matthew 5:17, *"Think not that I am come to destroy the law, or the prophets: I am not come to destroy, but to fulfill.*

Jesus not only fulfills the prophecies but also reveals the weakness of the laws through grace.

In Hebrews, Paul reiterated that, concerning the law being weak, Christ came as the channel of grace. The law that was given by Moses was not executed according to the intent of God's commandment. According to the law, the blood of bulls and goats was offered up year after year for sins. However, these sacrifices were made for sins continually, and a remembrance of sins was made every year. And it is impossible for the blood of bulls and goats to take away sins.

The emphasis was placed on carrying out the law so much that the praise and glory were not given to God. It was overshadowed by the literal execution of the law, highlighting the lawgiver and the commandments rather than the Creator.

Therefore, they were acted out as rituals. As a result, the spiritual factor of the law was not fulfilled in the hearts of men. This is reason why Jesus said, "I am not come to destroy the law or prophets but to fulfill."

Fulfill means "to put into effect," "to achieve," "to carry out," "to realize," or to make clear. Jesus continues to explain a few of the misconceptions of the Law by clarifying in **Matthew 5:21-48**.

Murder

21 "Ye have heard that it was said of them of old time, Thou shalt not kill, and whosoever shall kill shall be in danger of the judgment:

22 But I say unto you, That whosoever is angry with his brother without a cause shall be in danger of the judgment.

23 Therefore if thou bring thy gift to the altar, and there rememberest that thy brother hath ought against thee;

24 Leave there thy gift before the altar, and go thy way; first be reconciled to thy brother, and then come and offer thy gift."

Adultery

27" Ye have heard that it was said by them of old time, Thou shalt not commit adultery:

28 But I say unto you, That whosoever looketh on a woman to lust after her hath committed adultery with her already in his heart."

Divorce

31 "It hath been said, Whosoever shall put away his wife, let him give her a writing of divorcement:

32 But I say unto you, That whosoever shall put away his wife, saving for the cause of fornication,

causeth her to commit adultery: and whosoever shall marry her that is divorced committeth adultery."

Oath

33 "Again, ye have heard that it hath been said by them of old time, Thou shalt not forswear thyself, but shalt perform unto the Lord thine oaths:

34 But I say unto you, Swear not at all; neither by heaven; for it is God's throne:

35 Nor by the earth; for it is his footstool: neither by Jerusalem; for it is the city of the great King.

36 Neither shalt thou swear by thy head, because thou canst not make one hair white or black.

37 But let your communication be, Yea, yea; Nay, nay: for whatsoever is more than these cometh of evil."

Eye for an Eye

38" Ye have heard that it hath been said, An eye for an eye, and a tooth for a tooth:

39 But I say unto you, That ye resist not evil: but whosoever shall smite thee on thy right cheek, turn to him the other also.

40 And if any man will sue thee at the law, and take away thy coat, let him have thy cloak also.

41 And whosoever shall compel thee to go a mile, go with him twain.

42 Give to him that asketh thee, and from him that would borrow of thee turn not thou away."

Love for Enemies

43 "Ye have heard that it hath been said, Thou shalt love thy neighbour, and hate thine enemy.

44 But I say unto you, Love your enemies, bless them that curse you, do good to them that hate you, and pray for them which despitefully use you, and persecute you;

45 That ye may be the children of your Father which is in heaven: for he maketh his sun to rise on the evil and the good, and sendeth rain on the just and on the unjust.

46 For if ye love them which love you, what reward have ye? Do not even the publicans the same?

47 And if ye salute your brethren only, what do ye more than others? Do not even the publicans so?

48 Be ye therefore perfect, even as your Father which is in heaven is perfect."

As the scripture mentions in **Hebrews 10:1-4,** *"For the law having a shadow of good things to come, and not the very image of the things, can never with those sacrifices which they offered year by year continually make the comers thereunto perfect. For then, would they not have ceased to be offered? Because the worshippers, once purged, should have had no more conscience of sins. But in those sacrifices, there is a remembrance again made of sins every year. For it is not possible that the blood of bulls and of goats should take away sins."*

So, for this reason, Jesus came and charted the plan of salvation to redeem humanity from sin. He fulfilled the law and prophets through a grace offering of Himself as the prize for our redemption. He became the lamb slain from the foundation of the world, Hebrews 9 and 10.

Hebrews 9:28, *"So Christ was once offered to bear the sins of many; and unto them that look for him shall he appear the second time without sin unto salvation*

Hebrews 10:10, *"By the which will we are sanctified through the offering of the body of Jesus Christ once for all."*

Hebrews 9:26, *"For then must he often have suffered since the foundation of the world: but now once in the end of the world hath he appeared to put away sin by the sacrifice of himself."*

Hebrews 9:11, *"But Christ being come a high priest of good things to come, by a greater and more perfect tabernacle, not made with hands, that is to say, not of this building;"*

Hebrews 9:12, *"Neither by the blood of goats and calves, but by his own blood he entered in once into the holy place, having obtained eternal redemption for us."*

Hebrews 9:15-17, *"And for this cause, he is the mediator of the New Testament, that by means of death, for the redemption of the transgressions that were under the first testament, they which are called might receive the promise of eternal inheritance. For where a testament is, there must also, of necessity, be the death of the testator. For a testament is of force after men are dead: otherwise, it is of no strength at all while the testator liveth."*

Here, we understand that Jesus' coming will bring a perfect tabernacle, meaning a sanctuary or habitation not made with hands. The laws were written on a tablet of stone, not in the hearts of men. Jesus intended that the laws would be in the hearts of men.

For this reason, He became the mediator of the New Testament, using his death as the ultimate sacrifice to redeem humanity. However, before His death, there must be His birth.

God designed this plan before the foundation of the world. He knew man would have fallen. However, since He created man to be independent and self-sufficient, God's desire was not to build robots but to create humans willing to make decisions, good or bad, understanding that each decision has resulting consequences. Therefore, His plan of redemption, to transform humanity from sin and death, was already in place as He transcended time through eternity.

Jesus came into humanity through the womb of a virgin, in the form of a man, accomplishing the birth process that would precede His death to redeem us from sin. So, (the Old Testament) the old law was fulfilled, justified, or made right by Jesus Christ through grace by which His blood cleanses us from sin. Now that we understand the reason for His entry, let's examine His method of entry. Why did Jesus come that way? And this could be the most important revelation of His deity.

His deity was prophesied by Isaiah the prophet in **Isaiah 9:6**, *"For unto us a child is born, unto us a son is given: and the government shall be upon his shoulder: and his name shall be called; Wonderful, Counselor, The Mighty God, The everlasting Father.*

The Prince of Peace

"Of the increase of his government and peace, there shall be no end, upon the throne of David, and upon his kingdom, to order it, and to establish it with judgment and with justice from henceforth even forever. The zeal of the LORD of hosts will perform this."

"Unto us, a child is born" is a common act but not a common statement. A child is born every day, but unto us, a son is given is an uncommon act and statement."

Isaiah gave an affiliation unto us but not a name; he continued, *"Unto us, a son is given."*

This is also a strange statement: "A son is given" is not a common; Jesus is the only son given to us. He shall have power over kingdoms to order and establish with judgment and justice forever. These are other annotations to the name of Jesus.

Immanuel (God with Us)

Wonderful (God of Wonder)

Counselor (He understands all things)

The Mighty God (All Mighty God)

The Everlasting Father (Father of all)

The Prince of Peace (Savior)

Immanuel—God with us

Immanuel – is defined as God with Us. It is crystal clear that the scripture is saying that this child should be born not just to represent a Prophet, Priest, or Prince, but he is God with us, in the person of Jesus Christ.

According to John 4:24, God is a Spirit; the only way we can experience God with us is if He presents Himself as an angel or a visible person, one that can be seen and touched. As an angel, however, He would still be a superior being, not in the human form. Therefore, He could not associate himself with humanity or accomplish salvation in this form.
Jesus is the person in whom dwelt the Spirit of the Almighty God, which makes Him the Mighty God, the Everlasting Father, and the Prince of Peace. God with Us, God entering earth in the human form to dwell among us, was the only way to redeem humanity.

In the same way, we have a body and a spirit separable only by death. God is the spirit that dwells in the body of Jesus Christ, which makes them one! The difference is that God has ultimate power over everything-the body and spirit. He has the power to transition from body to spirit and vice versa. Jesus knew his disciples, and the people generally did not understand this; most of all, He wanted the disciples to understand.

He knew He was not known by mankind as He should be, and neither did they understand the mystery of His deity. This mystery refers to the divine nature of Jesus that was often hidden or misunderstood. While many saw Him as a prophet or a miracle worker, they struggled to grasp the deeper truth of His divine connection with God. Jesus' true essence was veiled to humanity, making His mission and identity a profound enigma for those around Him.

Jesus wanted His disciples to understand His deity by revealing Himself, so that they might understand who He is.

He was with them daily, and they perceived him as the Son of God, not in a spiritual or supernatural form but natural, so intending to reveal Himself, he asked, "Who do men say that I am?"

Chapter 2

Who Do Men Say I Am?

But who do you say I am? After the birth of Jesus, He grew up among his brethren at the age of twelve, and He amazed the doctors with his words of wisdom. Everyone who heard him speak, asking and answering questions, was amazed at his wisdom and understanding.

Luke 2:42, "And when he was twelve years old, they went up to Jerusalem after the custom of the feast.

43 And when they had fulfilled the days, as they returned, the child Jesus tarried behind in Jerusalem, and Joseph and his mother knew not of it.

44 But they, supposing him to have been in the company, went a day's journey, and they sought him among their kinsfolk and acquaintance.

45 And when they found him not, they turned back again to Jerusalem, seeking him.

46 And it came to pass that after three days, they found him in the temple, sitting in the midst of the doctors, both hearing them and asking them questions.

47 And all that heard him were astonished at his understanding and answers.

48 And when they saw him, they were amazed: and his mother said unto him, Son, why hast thou thus dealt with us? Behold, thy father and I have sought thee sorrowing.

49 And he said unto them, how is it that ye sought me? wist ye not that I must be about my Father's business?"

At twelve, Jesus told His parents that He was going about His Father's business, understanding that this mission to redeem humanity from sin was part of His Father's work. When the time had fully come, Jesus chose twelve disciples. The names of the twelve apostles are these: Simon, who is called Peter, and Andrew his brother; James the son of Zebedee, and John his brother; Philip and Bartholomew; Thomas, and Matthew the publican; James the son of Alphaeus, and Lebbaeus, whose surname was Thaddaeus; Simon the Canaanite, and Judas Iscariot, who also betrayed him.

Jesus went around healing the sick, casting out devils, raising the dead, and performing many other miracles among the people in the presence of his disciples'. So much that John proclaimed in the gospel, "and there were many other signs and miracles that Jesus did among his disciples not recorded in the Bible. There were so many that if they were recorded, not even the world itself could hold the book that would have been written." amazing!

John 20:30, *"And many other signs truly did Jesus in the presence of his disciples, which are not written in this book:"*

John 21:25, *"And there are also many other things which Jesus did, the which, if they should be written every one, I suppose that even the world itself could not contain the books that should be written. Amen."*

Jesus emphasized the importance of those who see what the disciples saw and experienced.
In St Luke 10:23-24

23 And he turned him unto his disciples, and said privately, Blessed are the eyes which see the things that ye see:

24 For I tell you, that many prophets and kings have desired to see those things which ye see, and have not seen them; and to hear those things which ye hear, and have not heard them.

Jesus' prophetic words are evident today around the world, indicating man's desire to understand him better.
Knowing what we know today, we wish they had sent us more of the daily interactions with Jesus, especially as they relate to his Deity and Powers. However, the words recorded by the apostles suffice for the day.
Had they known who Jesus was, they would have recorded more of his Godliness. As we all see in the Gospel, John was the only disciple who recorded the most about Jesus' deity. However, in his words I believe there is undeniable evidence that Jesus is God.
Even if the disciples had received the inspiration and recorded more about his deity, there would still be some controversy today regarding his Godliness. As this is a great mystery, according to

the Apostle Paul, in his letters, he reminded Timothy of the great controversy. We will analyze this mystery in the next chapter

At the appointed time, Jesus gave the disciples powers. **Matthew 10:1,** *"And when he had called unto him his twelve disciples, he gave them power against unclean spirits, to cast them out, and to heal all manner of sickness and all manner of disease."*

The fact that, Jesus could have given the disciples such power over spirits and healed all manner of diseases not some, but all clearly shows that there is something supernatural about Him. No mortal man could have done anything close to what Jesus did. Yet, throughout their time with Him, they did not know who He truly was. Had they understood, then they would have asked more questions about His deity.

Jesus himself expressed these words, *"No man knoweth who the Father is but the Son, and to whom the Son will reveal himself."*
Matthew 11:27 *"All things are delivered unto me of my Father: and no man knoweth the Son, but the Father; neither knoweth any man the Father,*

save the Son, and he to whomsoever the Son will reveal him."

This statement from Jesus clearly exposed the ignorance of man regarding His relationship with God the Father. It would seem rather strange that Jesus said, "No man knoweth the Father, but the Son! and no man knoweth the Son but the Father." Confirming that there is a general lack of knowledge in the world regarding the relationship between the Father and the Son".

Many people naturally perceive Jesus as having a natural son and father relationship however, their relationship transcends the natural.

Jesus said all things are delivered unto me of my Father! It is important to understand that Jesus said all things are delivered unto me "**of** my Father" not "**by** my Father" This means all powers, characteristics, forms, and likeness.

His disciples and others surrounding Him daily and seeing all the miracles He performed, one would think they should have known Him. They should have said in their hearts, 'What manner of man is this?' Furthermore, they should have realized

Jesus was not a normal man but someone uniquely and supernaturally special.

However, Jesus spoke about the revelation of His deity as it relates to God the Father and Son. No man knows the mystery of their relationship. Jesus, however, can reveal this mystery of the Father and the Son to whoever He will.

One may ask: 'Why to whomever He will?' Jesus himself said, "Whosoever shall follow Him must first believe." Things we do not believe are more challenging to accept. So, if we want to know Jesus, we must first believe He will reveal Himself. Jesus wants the disciples to understand who He is and the mystery of his deity, which He could not reveal to them in the natural manner but rather spiritual.

The Godhead is a spiritual concept, not natural; the scriptures said the natural man cannot understand spiritual things.

1 Corinthians 2:14, *"But the natural man receiveth not the things of the Spirit of God: for they are foolishness unto him: neither can he know them, because they are spiritually discerned."*

Consequently, to understand His deity, you must understand His spirituality.

Jesus knew for sure they did not understand the mystery of his deity, so He asked the question in Matthew 16:13, hoping they would be curious. "Whom do men say I, the Son of man, am?" The intent of the question was not to find out who other men thought He was; rather, it was intended to hear his disciples take on the matter of his deity. That's why Jesus asked the disciples after they had explained who other people said He was. He then asked, *"But whom do you say I am?"*

Matthew 16:13-23: *"When Jesus came into the coasts of Caesarea Philippi, he asked his disciples, saying, Whom do men say that I the Son of man am?*

14 And they said, Some say that thou art John the Baptist: some, Elias; and others, Jeremias, or one of the prophets.

15 He saith unto them, 'But whom say ye that I am?'

16 And Simon Peter answered and said, Thou art the Christ, the Son of the living God.

17 And Jesus answered and said unto him, Blessed art thou, Simon Barjona: for flesh and blood hath not revealed it unto thee, but my Father which is in heaven.

18 And I say also unto thee, that thou art Peter, and upon this rock I will build my church; and the gates of hell shall not prevail against it.

19 And I will give unto thee the keys of the kingdom of heaven: and whatsoever thou shalt bind on earth shall be bound in heaven: and whatsoever thou shalt loose on earth shall be loosed in heaven.

20 Then charged he his disciples that they should tell no man that he was Jesus the Christ.

21 From that time forth began Jesus to shew unto his disciples, how that he must go unto Jerusalem, and suffer many things of the elders and chief priests and scribes, and be killed, and be raised again the third day.

22 Then Peter took him and began to rebuke him, saying, "Be it far from thee, Lord: this shall not be unto thee."

23 But he turned, and said unto Peter, "Get thee behind me, Satan: thou art an offense unto me: for thou savourest not the things that be of God, but those that be of men."

Astonishing! Peter was just exalted, given so much power. Jesus gave him the keys of the Kingdom of Heaven and power to bind and release on Earth, and Heaven would be confirmed. Can you try to imagine the level of authority and power that Jesus gave Peter? He did not even understand what it meant to receive the keys of the Kingdom of Heaven and so many powers, followed by a sudden rebuke from Jesus.

Peter answered Jesus' question correctly. Indeed, He is Christ, the Son of the living God. However, if Peter had thought about the answer, he would have asked himself. How art thou the Son of the living God? And God is a spirit, and you are flesh and blood? Jesus knew he did not understand the interpretation of what he said because Peter still saw Jesus as the natural Son of God rather than spiritual. Immediately after answering the question, Peter received authority naturally and spiritually. Peter had the golden opportunity to question such powers and the reason for the keys of the Kingdom of Heaven, which merits a reasonable inquiry.

First, Jesus called Peter the Rock upon which he would build His Church, and the gates of hell shall not prevail against it.

Secondly, He said, "I will give unto thee the keys of the kingdom of heaven."

Thirdly, Powers and whatsoever thou shall bind on earth shall be bound in heaven: and whatsoever thou shall loose on earth shall be loosed in heaven.

After receiving all these powerful proclamations, spiritual and natural, if I were in Peter's position, I would ask questions like: "Lord, how can I accomplish this? What is the meaning of this? What is the meaning of the Keys of the Kingdom?"

Jesus wanted Peter to question the meaning of his promotion; instead, Peter ignored all that exaltation. He did not even ask one question about his sudden promotion or offer any form of gratitude. Instead, he was distracted by the later statement Jesus mentioned about being killed. He rebukes Jesus, even though He said He would rise again on the third day. And, Peter totally ignored Jesus' statement that He would return again from the dead. Instead, he was so focused on the trivialities rather than the infinite things.

Matthew 16:22-23, *"Then Peter took him and began to rebuke him, saying, Be it far from thee, Lord: this shall not be unto thee. But he turned, and said unto Peter, Get thee behind me, Satan: thou art an offence unto me: for thou savourest not the things that be of God, but those that be of men."*

Have you ever been in such a situation as Jesus, doing your best to help someone understand something significant, even mysterious? As in the case of Jesus, however, instead of seeing the big picture, they are concerned about trivialities. Just imagine you were in Peter's position. Jesus said, "Thou art Peter, and upon this rock, I will build my church, and the gates of hell shall not prevail against it.

And I will give unto thee the keys of the kingdom of heaven: and whatsoever thou shalt bind on earth shall be bound in heaven: and whatsoever thou shalt loose on earth shall be loosed in heaven."

What would you do or say? Even though Jesus had rebuked Peter sharply, He did not withdraw His words regarding His proclamation on him.

It was materialized in Acts 2:14 and 38 when He stood up with the keys of the Kingdom of Heaven and proclaimed to the people: *"Repent and be baptized every one of you, and he shall receive the gift of the Holy Ghost."*

Jesus knew the enemy planned to work very hard to distract Peter from seeing and understanding the great mission he needed accomplish.

Jesus wanted Peter and the other disciples to understand who He was, so He decided to do something else to convince them of His Deity. Jesus desired that his disciples, of all men, should know He is God in the flesh.

So, exactly six days later, Jesus called three of his disciples to follow Him to the mountain, as if to say, "Come follow me; I need to show you something." Jesus transfigured before them so they could see Him for who He truly is.

Matthew 17:1-13, "And after six days Jesus took Peter, James, and John, his brother, and bringeth them up into a high mountain apart,

2 And was transfigured before them: and his face did shine as the sun, and his raiment was white as the light.

3 And, behold, there appeared unto them Moses and Elias talking with him.

4 Then answered Peter, and said unto Jesus, Lord, it is good for us to be here: if thou wilt, let us make here three tabernacles; one for thee, and one for Moses, and one for Elias.

5 While he yet spake, behold, a bright cloud overshadowed them: and behold a voice out of the cloud, which said, This is my beloved Son, in whom I am well pleased; hear ye him.

6 And when the disciples heard it, they fell on their face, and were sore afraid.

7 And Jesus came and touched them, and said, Arise, and be not afraid.

8 And when they had lifted up their eyes, they saw no man, save Jesus only.

9 And as they came down from the mountain, Jesus charged them, saying, Tell the vision to no man, until the Son of man be risen again from the dead.

10 And his disciples asked him, saying, Why then say the scribes that Elias must first come?

11 And Jesus answered and said unto them, Elias truly shall first come, and restore all things.

12 But I say unto you, That Elias is come already, and they knew him not, but have done unto him whatsoever they listed. Likewise shall also the Son of man suffer of them.

13 Then the disciples understood that he spake unto them of John the Baptist.

Wow!! They finally understood something but still did not ask the right questions. Peter's response is captured in **Mark 9:4-7,** "And there appeared unto them Elias with Moses: and they were talking with Jesus. And Peter answered and said to Jesus, Master, it is good for us to be here: and let us make three tabernacles; one for thee, and one for Moses, and one for Elias. For he wist not what to say; for they were sore afraid. And there was a cloud that overshadowed them: and a voice came out of the cloud, saying, This is my beloved Son: hear him."

He did not know what to say because he was so afraid. So, Peter's response was not that of inspiration but of fear. Again, his response was in the form of a suggestion and not a question. It would seem to me that all these overwhelming experiences required a question. Simply, Lord, what meanest this?
The reason for the transfiguration was not so much about Elias or Moses; it was about Jesus, His deity, and His powers of omniscience, omnipotence, and omnipresence.
He showed the disciples his transient omnipresent characteristics, as he transcends time which allowed him to speak to Moses, who died in 1410 B.C., years before, and Elias (John the Baptist), who had recently died.
Peter could recognize Moses even though he had never seen him before. Yet he did not ask about that supernatural encounter; instead, he asked to

build three tabernacles, still thinking in the natural.

Peter, with his level of intelligence and faith in the master, could not understand the ultimate truth of Jesus' deity; neither could he realize how close he was to the supreme creator of life. If they had known or discovered, as we understand from the revelation of scriptures, how long the path of faith has to travel, they would have told us much more about the master, His interactions with them, and the things He did that reveal His deity.

As John mentioned, the miracles Jesus performed were so numerous that if recorded, the whole world could not contain the book.

John 21:25 *And there are also many other things which Jesus did, the which, if they should be written every one, I suppose that even the world itself could not contain the books that should be written. Amen.*

Reflecting on their lives and connection with Christ reveals an extraordinary opportunity for understanding. The apostles experienced His presence daily, heard His voice, looked into His eyes, walked beside Him, ate at His table, and witnessed His miracles, yet they did not fully grasp who He was. If only they had understood the profound reality before them.

However, of all the apostles, John uniquely perceived the true nature of Jesus' deity. Unlike the others, he recognized the significance of the transfiguration, seeing Jesus revealed as God.

Despite his outspokenness, Peter responded to the transfiguration from a practical perspective and did not explore its deeper spiritual meaning. John's silence was purposeful; he listened deeply and considered Jesus' teachings, seeking to understand every event's deeper meaning. The gospel of John begins with 'In the beginning,' powerfully expressing Jesus' oneness with God and aiming to reveal the underlying reality of His deity

In fact, there was no better way to express the oneness of God in Jesus than, "In the beginning." John wanted to take us back to where it all began.

Chapter 3

His Deity

In John chapter 1, John begins with the phrase "In the beginning," as Genesis starts with the exact words, "In the beginning." John wanted to reveal that Jesus was "the Word" and that Jesus was God in creation. In the beginning, it confirms that Jesus was with God in the beginning, not as two different individuals but as one.

1 John 5:7 references that the Word' bears record in heaven, emphasizing the oneness of God. The world sees this as a trinity; however, it represents his omnipotent power, transcending time.

"For there are three that bear record in heaven, the Father, the Word, and the Holy Ghost: and these three are one."

John explains that Jesus was the Word in the beginning with God, and he confirmed it all precisely in the first chapter of **John 1 1-3,**
"In the beginning was the Word, and the Word was with God, and the Word was God. John clearly indicated the Word was GOD. The same was the beginning with God.

He made all things; and without him was not anything made that made."

Furthermore, John confirms that all things were created by Him and without Him there was nothing made that existed, meaning all things were through Him and by Him. Throughout the New Testament, Jesus refers to Himself as the 'Son of Man.' If we replace instances of 'Word' with 'Son of Man' (both referring to Jesus), it will reveal the expression of John's words and read like this: "In the beginning, was the Son of man, and the Son of man was with God, and the Son of man was God." John could not make it any simpler than that; he expanded on the oneness by describing Jesus as the light.

John highlights that He came unto His own and His own received Him not. Since the disciples did not know Jesus as He truly was, He would not be known to the world. Today, over two thousand years later, people are still confused about His deity; however, this is not strange, considering it is a mystery.

John 1 4-10, *"In him was life, and the life was the light of men. Jesus came as a light to lighten all men.*

5 And the light shineth in darkness; and the darkness comprehended it not. There was a man sent from God, whose name was John.

7 The same came for a witness, to bear witness of the Light, that all men through him might believe.

8 He was not that Light, but was sent to bear witness of that Light.

9 That was the true Light, which lighteth every man that cometh into the world.

10 He was in the world, and the world was made by him, and the world knew him not.

11 He came unto his own, and his own received him not.

John 1:18, *"No man hath seen God at any time; the only begotten Son, which is in the bosom of the Father, he hath declared him."*

Jesus was in the world. He made the world, but even today, the world still does not know him. John again reemphasizes the world's ignorance of Jesus' deity. He created the world, yet the world does not know of him, even after all this overwhelming evidence; there are still people today who will not fathom the revelation of his deity.
Verses 10 and 11 may be paraphrased as fallows: Jesus was in the world, He made the world, and the world did not know Jesus.
Jesus came unto us, and we received him not. Here, we see the scripture highlights: God was in the world, the world was made by him, and the world knew him not. He came unto his own, and they received him not. John could only be referring to Jesus. John refers to Jesus as the Word from the beginning and that the Word was God.

John 1:14, *"And the Word was made flesh and dwelt among us, (and we beheld his glory, the glory as of the only begotten of the Father,) full of grace and truth."*

John reveals the most critical transformation of the Word. The Word was made flesh in the person of Jesus Christ and dwelt among us as a human.

However, we could not perceive or accept him as God, the creator of the universe, so we accepted Him as the only begotten Son of the Father, full of grace and truth.

John 13:31-32, *"Therefore, when he was gone out, Jesus said, Now is the Son of man glorified, and God is glorified in him. If God be glorified in him, God shall also glorify him in himself, and shall straightway glorify him."*

Here the scripture highlights the obsolete oneness of Jesus and God, Jesus clearly indicate that God is glorified in him. **And if God is glorified in him, God shall also glorify him in himself.** This statement is showing that God is referring to himself when he glorified Jesus, showing their absolute oneness.

John 14:1, *"Let not your heart be troubled: ye believe in God, believe also in me."*

Since Jesus and God are one, whoever believes in God believes also in Jesus.

John explains why this book was written in chapter 1, verse 31. *"But these are written, that ye might believe that Jesus is the Christ, the Son of God; and that believing ye might have life through his name."* Again, here we understand the revelation of God the Spirit in Christ Jesus. The Word, which is God the Spirit, was adorned with the flesh of Jesus Christ, which was already in the form and likeness and image of God.

John went back to the beginning to reveal the presence of God the Spirit with Jesus. **Genesis 1:1-4,** *"In the beginning, God created the heaven and the earth. And the earth was without form, and void; and darkness was upon the face of the deep. And the Spirit of God moved upon the face of the waters. And God said, Let there be light: and there was light. And God saw the light, that it was good: and God divided the light from the darkness."*

And God said, let there be light, and there was light; these were all "words" commanded by the Spirit of God, expressing His power and accomplishing His will. These "words" are what John refers to as the "Word." Jesus was "the Word" in the beginning; as John mentioned, all things were created by the expressed words. Jesus, the living and spoken Word! Jesus also mentioned in **John 6:63,** *"It is the spirit that quickeneth; the flesh profiteth nothing: the words that I speak unto you, they are spirit, and they are life."*

His Words Are Spirit and Life.

John indicated the Word (Jesus) was in the beginning with God when He said in **Genesis 1:26,** *"Let us make man after our image and likeness,"* it clearly shows that even though God is a Spirit, He already has an image and likeness of man, which is the expressed image of Jesus Christ.

Genesis 1:26-27, *"And God said, Let us make man in our image, after our likeness: and let them have dominion over the fish of the sea, and over the fowl of the air, and over the cattle, and over all the earth, and over every creeping thing that creepeth upon the earth. So, God created man in his own image, in the image of God created he him; male and female created he them."*

All of these are spoken words, and "God said" them! The Bible clearly states that God created the heavens and the earth; however, John said the earth was created by Jesus, and without Him, there was nothing made that was made. So, if God created the heavens and the earth, and Jesus did the same, they are not mutually exclusive—they are one and the same.

Isaiah 43:10, "Ye are my witnesses, saith the LORD, and my servant whom I have chosen: that ye may know and believe me, and understand that I am he: before me there was no God formed, neither shall there be after me."

Isaiah 43:15, "I am the LORD, your Holy One, the creator of Israel, your King."

On various occasions, while speaking to the people, including Jews, Jesus highlights his relationship with God the Father. However, on those occasions, they would pick up stones to stone him.

The Jews were convinced that Jesus did speak implicitly that He is God, they did not believe Him *mainly* because of their religious conviction, and the irony here is this should be the reason why they should have believed. As it was then, some religious people today adopt similar spirits of unbelief. However, even people today find it so difficult to understand who Jesus is. The Jews accused him of making Himself God. They simply refused to accept, in many ways, because of unbelief. Whereas the Jews chose not to believe, they understood what He was saying and chose to stone him, instead of asking him to explain so they could understand or just accept him as God.

John 10: 27-33, *"My sheep hear my voice, and I know them, and they follow me:*

28 And I give unto them eternal life, and they shall never perish, neither shall any man pluck them out of my hand.

29 My Father, which gave them me, is greater than all; and no man is able to pluck them out of my Father's hand.

30 I and my Father are one.

31 Then the Jews took up stones again to stone him.

32 Jesus answered them, 'Many good works have I shewed you from my Father; for which of those works do ye stone me?'

33 The Jews answered him, saying, 'For a good work we stone thee not; but for blasphemy; and because that thou, being a man, makest thyself God."

The Jews did perceived, that according to Jesus' teaching he was saying he is God. However, since they did not want to perceive him as God they said he was making himself God.

In Revelation, John also speaks of Jesus, seen not as the crucified savior but as King of Kings and the Great and only God, the Almighty. **Revelation 1:1-19** "The revelation of Jesus Christ, which God gave unto him, to shew unto his servants things which must shortly come to pass; and he sent and signified it by his angel unto his servant John:

2 Who bare record of the word of God, and of the testimony of Jesus Christ, and of all things that he saw.

3 Blessed is he that readeth, and they that hear the words of this prophecy, and keep those things which are written therein: for the time is at hand.

4 John to the seven churches which are in Asia: Grace be unto you, and peace, from him which is,

and which was, and which is to come; and from the seven Spirits which are before his throne;

5 And from Jesus Christ, who is the faithful witness, and the first begotten of the dead, and the prince of the kings of the earth. Unto him that loved us, and washed us from our sins in his own blood,

6 And hath made us kings and priests unto God and his Father; to him be glory and dominion forever and ever. Amen.

7 Behold, he cometh with clouds; and every eye shall see him, and they also which pierced him: and all kindreds of the earth shall wail because of him. Even so, Amen.

8 I am Alpha and Omega, the beginning and the ending, saith the Lord, which is, and which was, and which is to come, the Almighty.

9 I John, who also am your brother, and companion in tribulation, and in the kingdom and patience of Jesus Christ, was in the isle that is called Patmos, for the word of God, and for the testimony of Jesus Christ.

10 I was in the Spirit on the Lord's day, and heard behind me a great voice, as of a trumpet,

12 And I turned to see the voice that spake with me. And being turned, I saw seven golden candlesticks;

13 And in the midst of the seven candlesticks one like unto the Son of man, clothed with a garment down to the foot, and girt about the paps with a golden girdle.

14 His head and his hairs were white like wool, as white as snow; and his eyes were as a flame of fire;

15 And his feet like unto fine brass, as if they burned in a furnace; and his voice as the sound of many waters.

16 And he had in his right hand seven stars: and out of his mouth went a sharp two-edged sword: and his countenance [was] as the sun shineth in his strength.

17 And when I saw him, I fell at his feet as dead. And he laid his right hand upon me, saying unto me, Fear not; I am the first and the last:

18 I am he that liveth, and was dead; and, behold, I am alive for evermore, Amen; and have the keys of hell and of death.

19 Write the things which thou hast seen, and the things which are, and the things which shall be hereafter;"

Daniel also saw Him in a similar form hundreds of years (approximately 600 B.C.) before John. Their description was exactly the same. **Daniel 10:2-7,** "In those days I Daniel was mourning three full weeks.

3 I ate no pleasant bread, neither came flesh nor wine in my mouth, neither did I anoint myself at all, till three whole weeks were fulfilled.

4 And on the fourth and twentieth day of the first month, as I was by the side of the great river, which is Hiddekel;

5 Then I lifted up mine eyes, and looked, and behold a certain man clothed in linen, whose loins were girded with fine gold of Uphaz:

6 His body also was like the beryl, and his face as the appearance of lightning, and his eyes as lamps

of fire, and his arms and his feet like in colour to polished brass, and the voice of his words like the voice of a multitude.

7 And I Daniel alone saw the vision: for the men that were with me saw not the vision, but a great quaking fell upon them so that they fled to hide themselves.

God entering the world in human form to dwell among us was the only way to redeem humanity.

There are no other words that could define His Deity other than the Mighty God. Of whom Isaiah *prophesied hundreds of years* before the birth of Jesus. Now, there is no need for any controversy regarding His deity in the scriptures. However, as Paul indicated, it is a great mystery, and many may not understand it. He reminds us in his letter to Timothy, "And without controversy great is the mystery of godliness:"

Chapter 4

The Great Mystery of His Deity

Paul confirmed the mystery in his first epistle to Timothy in the third chapter and verse sixteen.

1 Timothy- 3:16, And without controversy, Great is the mystery of godliness: God was manifested in the flesh. Justified in the spirit, seen by Angels. Preached among the Gentiles, and received up in glory."

Although Paul admits that this is a great mystery, there was no need for controversy.
He understood that there would be some, so in his letter to Timothy, he begins by encouraging him not to dispute or deny Jesus's Deity. Let us thoroughly examine this.
Paul started this verse with an "and" as if it were a continuation of a prior statement; the verse above indicates, "The church of God is the living pillar of truth," and without controversy great is the mystery of godliness.

Paul knew this would cause some controversy, yet leaves no question in our minds that some people may not understand or simply refuse to accept the fact that this is not just a mystery but a great mystery.

Paul wrote to Timothy, saying that God was manifested in the flesh (God appearing in the form of flesh in the person of Jesus, the Son of Man). He also highlighted this when we read **Ephesians 3:4-5 and verse 9:** *How that by revelation he made known unto me the mystery; as I wrote afore in few words. "Which in other ages was not made known unto the sons of men, as it is now revealed unto his holy apostles and prophets by the Spirit;"*
9: And to make all men see what is the fellowship of the mystery, which from the beginning of the world hath been hid in God, who created all things by Jesus Christ:"
Paul just explained how the mystery of Jesus Christ, which was hidden in God from the beginning of the world, is now revealed. Therefore, God's eternal plan of salvation was hidden in Christ Jesus, which would be revealed at the time appointed.

Here, we understand that the world was blind to the revelation of Jesus Christ, as it hidden from the foundation of the world. However, it is now revealed to his holy apostles and prophets by the Holy Spirit.

Also, in **Colossians 1- 26**, *"Even the mystery which hath been hidden from ages and from generations, but now is made manifest to his saints:"*

This mystery is now revealed to you, do you believe?

Furthermore, in **Colossians 2: 8 and 9**, Paul reminds us to;

⁸ Beware lest any man spoil you through philosophy and vain deceit, after the tradition of men, after the rudiments of the world, and not after Christ.

⁹ For in him dwelleth all the fulness of the Godhead bodily.

For in Christ dwelleth all the fullness of the Godhead bodily.

Paul is saying here that the deity dwelleth in Christ himself bodily. But now this is revealed to you, I do believe! Will you believe it? Remember the devil himself believe and tremble.

James 2:19 *Thou believest that there is one God; thou doest well: the devils also believe, and tremble.*

In **2 Corinthians 5:19,** *"To wit, that God was in Christ, reconciling the world unto himself, not imputing their trespasses unto them; and hath committed unto us the word of reconciliation."*

Paul keeps reiterating the mystery of Christ in God; here, he said this mystery of His deity had been hidden in God from the beginning, Jesus with God from creation, the beginning, when He created all things, not as two separate individuals but as one. Paul encourages Timothy to accept this without controversy.

Now, there are many questions one could ask, but this is a mystery, so let us analyze this mystery. **Here is the first part of the mystery: God is a Spirit and God was manifested in the flesh, in human form Jesus Christ.**

Found in **John 4:24** *"God is a Spirit: and they who worship him must worship him in spirit and in truth."*

God is a spirit, and a spirit cannot be seen or touched by men physically, so this spirit, which is God, puts on flesh and becomes human—Jesus (God with us). In the same way, each one of us, humans, has a spirit and a body; our body cannot function without our spirit. And this is the same way Jesus' indwelling Spirit is God the Father. God is a Spirit, and we cannot separate the body from the spirit— they are one. The body cannot function without the spirit.

The Spirit and Body

The scripture says in **James 2:26,** *"For as the body without the spirit is dead, so faith without works is dead also."* The body is the actual clothing or frame for the spirit, but they have to work in unison, for one cannot function without the other.

Jesus clarifies this by saying *He is in the Father* and the *Father is in Him*, specifying that *God dwells in Him, and He in God*—since they are one. And He can do nothing of Himself but the spirit that is in Him doeth all the works.

John 14:10, *"Believest thou not that I am in the Father, and the Father in me? the words that I speak unto you I speak not of myself: but the Father that dwelleth in me, he doeth the works."*

During Jesus' crucifixion, the Bible explains how He yelled and yielded up the spirit, which was the only time God the Spirit departed from Him. So, He, the flesh, as a human man, cried out: "My God! My God! Why hast thou forsaken me?" Now, let us analyze the second part of this great mystery.

The second part of this mystery—"No man has seen God at any time."

Paul said he was seen by angels, but no one has seen God at any time. ***John 1:18,*** *"No man hath seen God at any time; the only begotten Son, which is in the bosom of the Father, he hath declared him."*

Jesus did not at any time explicitly declare Himself as God, saying, "I am God," as this would contradict the Bible. He referred to himself as the Son of Man. Also, man in his sinful flesh cannot look upon the intensity of the radiance of the power of almighty God. God in his Godly form cannot be fathomed by man. Man cannot look upon him in his holiness, power, and great glory. Jesus did try to reveal Himself to the disciples in a small fraction of His radiant power. However, He had to overshadow them with a cloud, as they could not endure the intensity of His brightness, which was like the sun.

Matthew 17:5-8, *While he yet spake, behold, a bright cloud overshadowed them: and behold, a voice out of the cloud, which*

said, this is my beloved Son, in whom I am well pleased; hear ye him.

6 And when the disciples heard it, they fell on their face and were sore afraid.

7 And Jesus came and touched them, and said, Arise, and be not afraid.

8 And when they had lifted up their eyes, they saw no man, save Jesus only."

Also, Saul, who was renamed Paul, experienced his radiant power like the brightness of the sun while he was on his way to Damascus to persecute the Christians. As a result, he was blinded for three days.

Acts 9:3-9, *"And as he journeyed, he came near Damascus: and suddenly there shined round about him a light from heaven:*

4 And he fell to the earth, and heard a voice saying unto him, Saul, Saul, why persecutest thou me?

5 And he said, Who art thou, Lord? And the Lord said, I am Jesus whom thou persecutest: it is hard for thee to kick against the pricks.

6 And he trembling and astonished said, Lord, what wilt thou have me to do? And the Lord said unto him, Arise, and go into the city, and it shall be told thee what thou must do.

7 And the men which journeyed with him stood speechless, hearing a voice, but seeing no man.

8 And Saul arose from the earth; and when his eyes were opened, he saw no man: but they led him by the hand, and brought him into Damascus.

9 And he was three days without sight, and neither did eat nor drink."

Saul asked, "Who art thou, Lord? As he realized that this experience was supernatural, the experience on the road to Damascus allowed him to receive the revelation of Jesus Christ, whom he had persecuted. We will examine the various transformations God undertakes to accomplish humanity's redemption. The scriptures continue with an exception, however: no man has seen God, except the only begotten Son; He has declared Him. So, Jesus revealed the mighty God! Not in His radiant power as He is, but in the actual human likeness that He took on. However, he has the power to transform into his Godly form.

How did Jesus declare him? Let's see what Jesus said in **John 14:1,** "*Let not your heart be troubled: ye believe in God, believe also in me.*"

John 10:30, "*I and my Father are one.*

Since Jesus and God are one, then if we believe in one, then we believe in the other."

Thomas was also curious and wanted to understand more about Jesus, as He continued to speak in **John 14:4-7**, "*And whither I go ye know, and the way ye know.*

5 Thomas saith unto him, Lord, we know not whither thou goest; and how can we know the way?

6 Jesus saith unto him, I am the way, the truth, and the life: no man cometh unto the Father but by me.

7 If ye had known me, ye should have known my Father also: and from henceforth ye know him, and have seen him."

Now, verse seven must have been the closest Jesus ever came to revealing Himself to the disciples as the Mighty God, the Everlasting Father. Jesus said, "If you know me, then you should have known my Father also!" And here is the revealing statement. "And henceforth," meaning, from this moment on, you **know Him** and not only know him but have **seen Him** ! There were no other words or adjectives to make this a clearer statement to the disciples.

Yet, Phillip requires further clarification and description of the Father, so he asks Jesus another question. Jesus then asked Phillip a more revealing question.

John 14:8-11, *"Philip saith unto him, Lord, shew us the Father, and it sufficeth us.*
9 Jesus saith unto him, have I been so long time with you, and yet hast thou not known me, Philip?

He that hath seen me hath seen the Father; and how sayest thou then, Shew us the Father? Believest thou not that I am in the Father, and the Father in me? ***the words that I speak unto you I speak not of myself: but the Father that dwelleth in me, he doeth the works.****"*

This verse expresses more clearly that God the Father, who is the Spirit, dwelleth in Jesus, the person. Jesus also explains that He can do nothing of Himself, but the Father, who dwells in Him, does the work. As mentioned before, the same way that we have a body and a spirit, the body without the spirit is dead, and without the spirit that dwells in us, we can do nothing.

Like Jesus said, *"Believe me that I am in the Father, and the Father in me: or else believe me for the very works' sake."*

Here, Jesus was using all possible means to convince Philip so he could believe that He was God in the flesh. So, as a means of recognizing that, He said to Phillip, *"If you do not believe me, just believe because of the works that you have seen accomplished by my hands.*

Miracles like the dead raised, the dumb speak, the lame walk, the blind see, the sick healed, and more."

Jesus was clearly saying here that God the Spirit, which is the Father, dwells in Him. As every human consists of a spirit and a body, our physical body does nothing unless the indwelling spirit powers us to walk, talk, move, etc.

This is how Jesus declared the Father; the Spirit of the Father dwells in Him, and He can do nothing of Himself except the Father who dwells in Him. Jesus expresses his oneness with God the Father: 'I can do nothing of Myself.' The words you hear are not of Myself but the Spirit of the Father who dwells in me to do the works.

Just imagine your body without the spirit. Your body can do nothing without the spirit; a body without the spirit is dead. In the same way, Jesus explains to Thomas, Phillip, and the other disciples that the Spirit dwells in us and manages and orders all the operations of the human body.

We cannot move, speak, or use any of our senses without the spirit in us. It would be contrary to Scripture if Jesus had revealed Himself as God, as it was prophesied by the prophets that no man can see him and live.

Exodus 33-20, *"There shall no man see me and live. This was also confirmed in* ***John chapter 1, verse 18,*** *"No man has seen God at any time. The Only begotten Son Who is in the bosom of the Father HE HATH DECLARE HIM..."*

Jesus represents the very God incarnate while on earth. He was flesh, human, but the spirit (which is God) that dwells in Him.

The flesh (human) cried out on the cross when the spirit left, so He would experience death.

With His last breath, He cried, *"My lord, why hast thou forsaken me?"* The spiritual connection between them was at a higher level than a man could ever comprehend, yet in a manner similar to humans. Jesus is the Lamb slain from the foundation of the world. The birth, death, and resurrection of Jesus were not a historic incident. It was by his design in the master's plan.

Hebrews 9:26, *"For then must he often have suffered since the foundation of the world: but now once in the end of the world hath he appeared to put away sin by the sacrifice of himself."*

Third, part of the mystery – I and my Father are one.

Now this may be the greatest part of this mystery.

Chapter 5

My Father and I Are One

John 10 25-31, *"Jesus answered them, I told you, and ye believed not: the works that I do in my Father's name, they bear witness of me.*

26 But ye believe not, because ye are not of my sheep, as I said unto you.

27 My sheep hear my voice, and I know them, and they follow me:

28 And I give unto them eternal life, and they shall never perish, neither shall any man pluck them out of my hand.

29 My Father, which gave them me, is greater than all; and no man is able to pluck them out of my Father's hand.

30 I and my Father are one.

31 Then the Jews took up stones again to stone him."

Jesus highlights the statement about Himself and God the Father to his followers to show their oneness. He said, "*My sheep know my voice, and they follow me, and I give unto them eternal life.*" (The Father alone gives eternal life). "My Father, who gives them to Me, is greater than all; and no man can pluck them out of my Father's hand." This scripture confirms that Jesus' hand and the Father's hand must be the same, as revealed in verse thirty, emphasizing His oneness.

Jesus tells them the truth, and they don't like it; they did not want to believe it, but still, they ask for the truth. They said, "Tell us plainly, Jesus." He honored their request, and again, they took up stones to stone him.

Ironically, almost everything Jesus did was offensive to the Jews. They said He made Himself out to be God, their Creator, whom they refused to accept.

When prophecy promised a deliverer of the Jews, Jesus was not the deliverer they expected. As scripture indicates, He came unto His own, and His own received Him not. Yet many people today, including Jews, still refuse to accept Jesus, our Creator, Redeemer, and Savior.

1 John 10:32-33, *"Jesus answered them, "Many good works have I shewed you from my Father; for which of those works do ye stone me? The Jews answered him, saying, For a good work we stone thee not; but for blasphemy; and because that thou, being a man, makest thyself God."*

Here, we understand that, even though Jesus did not say, 'I am God,' From these statements, the Jews understood that He was claiming to be God. However, the Jews could not perceive the concept of his deity and his relationship with God. So, rather than trying to understand, they bluntly refused and called Jesus a blasphemer.

1 John 5:1-21, *"Whosoever believeth that Jesus is the Christ is born of God: and everyone that loveth him that begat loveth him also that is begotten of him.*

2 By this we know that we love the children of God, when we love God, and keep his commandments.

3 For this is the love of God, that we keep his commandments: and his commandments are not grievous.

4 For whatsoever is born of God overcometh the world: and this is the victory that overcometh the world, even our faith.

5 Who is he that overcometh the world, but he that believeth that Jesus is the Son of God?

6 This is he that came by water and blood, even Jesus Christ; not by water only, but by water and blood. And it is the Spirit that beareth witness, because the Spirit is truth.

7 For there are three that bear record in heaven, the Father, the Word, and the Holy Ghost: and these three are one.

8 And there are three that bear witness in earth, the Spirit, and the water, and the blood: and these three agree in one.

9 If we receive the witness of men, the witness of God is greater: for this is the witness of God which he hath testified of his Son.

10 He that believeth on the Son of God hath the witness in himself: he that believeth not God hath made him a liar; because he believeth not the record that God gave of his Son.

11 And this is the record, that God hath given to us eternal life, and this life is in his Son.

12 He that hath the Son hath life; and he that hath not the Son of God hath not life.

13 These things have I written unto you that believe on the name of the Son of God; that ye may know that ye have eternal life, and that ye may believe on the name of the Son of God.

14 And this is the confidence that we have in him, that, if we ask any thing according to his will, he heareth us:

15 And if we know that he hears us, whatsoever we ask, we know that we have the petitions that we desired of him.

16 If any man see his brother sin a sin which is not unto death, he shall ask, and he shall give him life for them that sin not unto death. There is a sin unto death: I do not say that he shall pray for it.

17 All unrighteousness is sin: and there is a sin not unto death.

18 We know that whosoever is born of God sinneth not; but he that is begotten of God keepeth himself, and that wicked one toucheth him not.

19 And we know that we are of God, and the whole world lieth in wickedness.

20 And we know that the Son of God is come, and hath given us an understanding, that we may know him that is true, and we are in him that is true, even in his Son Jesus Christ. This is the true God, and eternal life.

21 Little children, keep yourselves from idols. Amen

Mark also records the oneness of God; in **Mark 12:29,** "And Jesus answered him, The first of all the commandments is, Hear, O Israel; The Lord our God is one Lord.

Mark 12:32, "And the scribe said unto him, Well, Master, thou hast said the truth: for there is one God; and there is none other but he:"

Paul highlighted his oneness of Jesus; in **1 Corinthians 8:6,** "But to us there is but one God, *the Father, of whom are all things, and we in him; and one Lord Jesus Christ, by whom are all things, and we by him."*

John also revealed the oneness of Jesus in John 1:3, *"All things were made by him, and without him was not anything made that was made."* This means Jesus created the world. However, the Bible also says God created the heavens and the earth. Is the Bible contradicting itself? No! Rather, it is giving clarity revealing the oneness of Jesus and God. They both created this great heaven and earth, making them one and the same creator. As Jesus stated, "I and my Father are one." Isaiah also records his oneness in **Isaiah 43:10,** *"Ye are my witnesses, saith the LORD, and my servant whom I have chosen: that ye may know and believe me, and understand that I am he: before me there was no God formed, neither shall there be after me."*

Paul reminds us again in **Ephesians 4:4-6**, *"There is one body, and one Spirit, even as ye are called in one hope of your calling; One Lord, one faith, one baptism, One God and Father of all, who is above all, and through all, and in you all."*

And continue in **James 2:19,** "Thou believest that there is one God; thou doest well: the devils also believe, and tremble." Even the devil believes this fact and trembles. Jesus was not born according to the will and understanding of man.

John 1:13, "Which were born, not of blood, nor of the will of the flesh, nor of the will of man, but of God."

The scripture relates to Jesus and God the Father differently, as if they are different individuals. Jesus refers to Himself as the Son of man. However, this relates to the different representations in time, since God is a Spirit and He is omnipresent, as it relates to his role as he transcends time.

Jesus is God in creation, Son in redemption, and the Holy Spirit in regeneration, who is with us today. He could not have represented Himself as the mighty God to anyone; not only that, it would be a contradiction to the scriptures, and no one would have accepted Him.

This was confirmed in the scripture according to **John 8:56-59,** "When Jesus said; *Before Abraham* was I am. Your father Abraham rejoiced to see my day, and he saw it and was glad.

57 Then said the Jews unto him, Thou art not yet fifty years old, and hast thou seen Abraham?

58 Jesus said unto them, Verily, verily, I say unto you, "Before Abraham was, I am."

59 Then took they up stones to cast at him: but Jesus hid himself, and went out of the temple, going through the midst of them, and so passed by.

In another scripture, **John 5:18,** "Therefore the Jews sought the more to kill him, because he not only had broken the Sabbath, but said also that God was his Father, making himself equal with God."

Further in the same chapter, we find **John 5:43,** "I am come in my Father's name, and ye receive me not: if another shall come in his own name, him ye will receive." What Jesus does here is to confirm He and His Father are one. The Father's name is (Yeshua) Jesus.

John 5:45-47, *"Do not think that I will accuse you to the Father: there is one that accuseth you, even Moses, in whom ye trust. For had ye believed Moses, ye would have believed me: for he wrote of me. But if ye believe not his writings, how shall ye believe my words?"*

John 14:10, *"Believest thou not that I am in the Father, and the Father in me? The words that I speak unto you I speak not of myself: but the Father that dwelleth in me, he doeth the works."*

These scriptures unequivocally show the relationship between Jesus and the Father as one. He explained that the Father (God the Spirit) who dwells in Him accomplished the work. Remember, the devil himself believes and trembles. Do you?

Jesus explained how they trusted Moses more than He, the creator of the world. And even though they trusted Moses, they still did not believe his words. If they had, they would have believed Jesus, because Moses wrote about Him. Jesus replied to the Jews, in verse 58, before Abraham, 'I am' (Ehyeh), emphasizing His perpetual existence. Jesus could have said, "I was before Abraham." However, He said before

Abraham, *'I am'* also signifies that He was the *'I am'* Moses spoke to in the burning bush.

In **Exodus 3-14-15,** God said, *"And God said unto Moses, I AM THAT I AM: and he said, Thus shalt thou say unto the children of Israel, I AM hath sent me unto you. And God said moreover unto Moses, Thus shalt thou say unto the children of Israel, the LORD God of your fathers, the God of Abraham, the God of Isaac, and the God of Jacob, hath sent me unto you: this is my name forever, and this is my memorial unto all generations."*

God revealed His name to Moses while in the burning bush; however, Moses could not comprehend the response, *'I am that I am.'* Tell the children of Israel, 'I AM' have sent you, then he went on to clarify, saying unto the children of Israel, that; the God of your fathers, the God of Isaac, the God of Jacob is my name forever; this is my memorial unto all generations. This is a pivotal moment where God reveals to Moses that He is the "I AM" that name is associated with the God of Isaac, the God of Jacob, even unto Jesus—the "I AM Jesus said unto the Jews before Abraham existed "I AM "(Yahweh) "Yeshua" (Jesus) Savior.

God reveals himself in diverse forms to his people throughout generations, as he transcends time to accomplish his Divine plan of salvation.

As Paul expressed in **Hebrews 1:1-2,** *"God, who at sundry times and in divers manners spake in time past unto the fathers unto the prophets, Hath in these last days spoken to us by his Son, whom he hath appointed heir of all things, by whom also he made the worlds."*

The Bible expresses in many deliberate scriptures the ones of God and Jesus, emphasizing their divine relationship as God the only savior and Jesus the savior.

Chapter 6

God, Our Only Savior—Jesus, the Only Savior

Jesus came as the Savior and redeemer of the world; He died to redeem humanity. In Isaiah, the word of God to Isaiah the Prophet often indicated that God is our redeemer and the only Savior. There are various unique comparisons in the scriptures concerning Jesus' deity and His relationship with God, the Father.

The Word of God shows in **Isaiah 43:11,** *"I, even I, am the Lord and beside me, there is no savior."*

Isaiah 43:3, *"For I am the LORD thy God, the Holy One of Israel, thy Saviour: I gave Egypt for thy ransom, Ethiopia and Seba for thee."*

In **Matthew 1:21**, the scripture indicates Jesus would save His people from their sins.

Christ Jesus, A Savior

Luke 2:11, *"For unto you is born this day in the city of David a Saviour, which is Christ the Lord."* The

Word of God in Isaiah declares the association with God the Almighty and Jesus Christ, our Savior. The scripture says, *"I, even I am the Lord, and beside me, there is no savior."* Showing the oneness of God, the only Savior, and Christ our Lord. When Paul wrote to Titus regarding Jesus' deity, it was not to suggest that they were separate individuals, but rather one and the same.

Titus 2:13, "*Looking for the blessed hope and the appearing of the glory of our great God and Savior, Christ Jesus:* Paul refers to Jesus as God and Savior, meaning He is our God and our Savior. As the words of God revealed in Isaiah,"

Isaiah 45:21, *"Tell ye, and bring them near; yea, let them take counsel together: who hath declared this from ancient time? Who hath told it from that time? Have not I the LORD? And there is no God else beside me; a just God and a Saviour; there is none beside me."*

Isaiah 43:15 says, *"I am the LORD, your Holy One, the creator of Israel, your King."*

The scriptures below indicate God and Savior, the Holy One, God the Creator, and God the King. However, when the Bible refers to **God and**

Saviour, it does not mean two different individuals but one individual with other attributes or qualities because He is God and our Savior, Jesus Christ one.

Luke 1:47, *"And my spirit hath rejoiced in God my Saviour."*

Ephesians 5:23, *"For the husband is the head of the wife, even as Christ is the head of the church: and he is the saviour of the body."*

Philippians 3:20, *"For our conversation is in heaven; from whence also we look for the Saviour, the Lord Jesus Christ:"*

1 Timothy 1:1, *"Paul, an apostle of Jesus Christ by the commandment of God our Saviour, and Lord Jesus Christ, which is our hope;"*

1 Timothy 2:3, *"For this is good and acceptable in the sight of God our Saviour;"*

1 Timothy 4:10, *"For therefore we both labour and suffer reproach, because we trust in the living God, who is the Saviour of all men, specially of those that believe."*

2 Timothy 1:10, "But is now made manifest by the appearing of our Saviour Jesus Christ, who hath abolished death, and hath brought life and immortality to light through the gospel:"

In Titus 1:3-4, "But hath in due times manifested his word through preaching, which is committed unto me according to the commandment of God our Saviour; To Titus, mine own son after the common faith: Grace, mercy, and peace, from God the Father and the Lord Jesus Christ our Saviour."

1 John 4:14, "And we have seen and do testify that the Father sent the Son to be the Saviour of the world."

Titus 2:10, "Not purloining, but shewing all good fidelity; that they may adorn the doctrine of God our Saviour in all things."

Titus 2:13, "Looking for that blessed hope, and the glorious appearing of the great God and our Saviour Jesus Christ;"

2 Peter 1:11, "For so an entrance shall be ministered unto you abundantly into the everlasting kingdom of our Lord and Saviour Jesus Christ."

2 Peter 3:18, *"But grow in grace, and in the knowledge of our Lord and Saviour Jesus Christ. To him be glory both now and forever. Amen."*

Jude 1:25, *"To the only wise God our Saviour, be glory and majesty, dominion and power, both now and ever. Amen."*

CHAPTER 7

God Our Redeemer— Jesus Our Redeemer

Jesus is the Savior and Redeemer of the world who died to redeem humanity. Here are a few scriptures that show the occasions where God is our Redeemer and the only Savior.

Isaiah 44:6, "Thus saith the LORD the King of Israel, and his redeemer the LORD of hosts; I am the first, and I am the last; and beside me there is no God."

Isaiah 44:8, "Fear ye not, neither be afraid: have not I told thee from that time, and have declared it? ye are even my witnesses. Is there a God beside me? yea, there is no God; I know not any."

Job 19:23-25, "Oh that my words were now written! Oh, that they were printed in a book! That they were graven with an iron pen and lead in the rock forever! For I know that my redeemer liveth, and that he shall stand at the latter day upon the earth:"

In the earliest book of the Bible, Job prophesied about God standing on the earth in the latter days in the form of Jesus. Why did Job mention this? With whom was Job associating God when he said, His Redeemer! Why would he stand on the earth in the latter days? Job could only be talking about Jesus (Yeshua). This prophecy is unrelated to Job's suffering. However, in Job's response to his companions and their negative perspective of his condition, there was a sudden change in his voice.

Even in Job's suffering and criticism, he was able to see beyond his circumstances. What he saw in the spirit was his Redeemer standing on the earth in the latter days. The scriptures below highlight the oneness of God, our Redeemer, and Jesus, our Redeemer.

Psalms 19:14, *"Let the words of my mouth, and the meditation of my heart, be acceptable in thy sight, O LORD, my strength, and my redeemer."*

Psalms 78:35, *"And they remembered that God was their rock, and the high God their redeemer."*

Proverb 23:11, *"For their redeemer is mighty; he shall plead their cause with thee."*

Isaiah 44:6, *"Thus saith the LORD the King of Israel, and his redeemer the LORD of hosts; I am the first, and I am the last; and beside me there is no God."*

Isaiah 44:24, *"Thus saith the LORD, thy redeemer, and he that formed thee from the womb, I am the LORD that maketh all things; that stretcheth forth the heavens alone; that spreadeth abroad the earth by myself;"*

Isaiah 47:4, *"As for our redeemer, the LORD of hosts is his name, the Holy One of Israel."*

Isaiah 54:5, *"For thy Maker is thine husband; the LORD of hosts is his name; and thy Redeemer the Holy One of Israel; The God of the whole earth shall he be called."*

Isaiah 54:8, *"In a little wrath I hid my face from thee for a moment; but with everlasting kindness will I have mercy on thee, saith the LORD thy Redeemer."*

Isaiah 59:20, *"And the Redeemer shall come to Zion, and unto them that turn from transgression in Jacob, saith the LORD."*

Isaiah 63:16, *"Doubtless thou art our father, though Abraham be ignorant of us, and art our father, our redeemer; thy name is from everlasting."*

Jeremiah 50:34, *"Their Redeemer is strong; the LORD of hosts is his name: he shall thoroughly plead their cause, that he may give rest to the land, and disquiet the inhabitants of Babylon."*

The Bible reiterates that God is the only Savior and Redeemer in many different ways. Also, it indicates that Jesus is the only Savior and Redeemer. These deliberate scriptures highlight the undeniable oneness of Jesus with God.

Jesus was observed in the fiery furnace by King Nebuchadnezzar hundreds of years before His birth, as recorded in the Book of Daniel, chapter 3.

Daniel 3:19-25, *"Then was Nebuchadnezzar full of fury, and the form of his visage was changed against Shadrach, Meshach, and Abednego: therefore, he spake, and commanded that they should heat the furnace one seven times more than it was wont to be heated.*

And he commanded the most mighty men that were in his army to bind Shadrach, Meshach, and Abednego, and to cast them into the burning fiery furnace.

Then these men were bound in their coats, their hosen, their hats, and their other garments and were cast into the midst of the burning fiery furnace.

Therefore, because the king's commandment was urgent, and the furnace exceeding hot, the flame of the fire slew those men that took up Shadrach, Meshach, and Abednego. And these three men, Shadrach, Meshach, and Abednego, fell down bound into the midst of the burning fiery furnace. Then Nebuchadnezzar the king was astonished, rose up in haste, spake, and said unto his counselors, Did not we cast three men bound into the midst of the fire? They answered and said unto the king, True, O king. He answered and said, Lo, I see four men loose, walking in the midst of the fire, and they have no hurt; **and the form of the fourth is like the Son of God."**

This is very strange. How could Nebuchadnezzar identify the fourth person as *"...like unto the Son of God?"*

There was no mention of the Son of God before, except for referring to Jesus in the New Testament.

This was the only occasion in the Old Testament in which someone was described as the Son of God hundreds of years before the birth of Jesus.

How and why did Nebuchadnezzar recognize the fourth person in the furnace as the Son of God? Why not like the Spirit of God, an angel, or just a spirit? The person that Nebuchadnezzar saw was not just a spirit or an angel.

Nebuchadnezzar observed that His form and likeness were unnatural; his appearance was like some supernatural being, and this description was a divine revelation.

This also confirms that Jesus is from the beginning and is the image God took on to Himself from the beginning of the world, as mentioned in the scriptures. Jesus is the expressed image of God!

Hebrews 1:1-3, *"God, who at sundry times and in divers manners spake in time past unto the fathers by the prophets, Hath in these last days spoken unto us by his Son, whom he hath appointed heir of all things, by whom also he made the worlds; Who being the brightness of his glory, and the express image of his person, and upholding all things by the word of his power, when he had by himself purged our sins, sat down on the right hand of the Majesty on high.*

He was in the world, The world was made by him, and the world knew him not! He came unto his own, and his own received him not."

John 1:12-17, *But as many as received him, to them gave he power to become the sons of God, even to them that believe on his name: Which were born, not of blood, nor of the will of the flesh, nor the will of man, but of God.*

And of his fullness have all we received, and grace for grace. For the law was given by Moses, but grace and truth came by Jesus Christ."

Hundreds of years before the birth and crucifixion of Jesus, Isaiah prophesied this. **Isaiah 53:3-12,** *"He is despised and rejected of men; a man of* sorrows, and acquainted with grief: and we hid as it were our faces from him; he was despised, and we esteemed him not.

4 Surely he hath borne our griefs, and carried our sorrows: yet we did esteem him stricken, smitten of God, and afflicted.

5 But he was wounded for our transgressions, he was bruised for our iniquities: the chastisement of our peace was upon him; and with his stripes we are healed.

6 All we like sheep have gone astray; we have turned every one to his own way; and the LORD hath laid on him the iniquity of us all.

7 He was oppressed, and he was afflicted, yet he opened not his mouth: he is brought as a lamb to the slaughter, and as a sheep before her shearers is dumb, so he openeth not his mouth.

8 He was taken from prison and from judgment: and who shall declare his generation? for he was cut off out of the land of the living: for the transgression of my people was he stricken.

9 And he made his grave with the wicked, and with the rich in his death; because he had done no violence, neither was any deceit in his mouth.

10 Yet it pleased the LORD to bruise him; he hath put him to grief: when thou shalt make his soul an offering for sin, he shall see his seed, he shall prolong his days, and the pleasure of the LORD shall prosper in his hand.

11 He shall see of the travail of his soul, and shall be satisfied: by his knowledge shall my righteous servant justify many; for he shall bear their iniquities.

12 Therefore will I divide him a portion with the great, and he shall divide the spoil with the strong; because he hath poured out his soul unto death: and he was numbered with the transgressors; and he bears the sin of many, and made intercession for the transgressors."

The prophecy was fulfilled in the books of the New Testament hundreds of years after Isaiah prophesied it. Isaiah expresses Jesus' painful journey, highlighting the path to the cross, the path of sorrow. He was despised and rejected by men; a man of sorrow acquainted with grief.

Throughout Jesus' journey, He was rejected and despised by the Jews, Kings, friends, Pharisees, Sadducees, Priests, and even His disciples.

Matthew 27:20-26, *"But the chief priests and elders persuaded the multitude that they should ask Barabbas, and destroy Jesus. 21 The governor answered and said unto them, 'Whether of the twain will ye that I release unto you?' They said, 'Barabbas.'*

22 Pilate saith unto them, What shall I do then with Jesus which is called Christ? They all say unto him, Let him be crucified.

23 And the governor said, Why, what evil hath he done? But they cried out the more, saying, Let him be crucified.

24 When Pilate saw that he could prevail nothing, but rather a tumult was made, he took water and washed his hands before the multitude, saying, I am innocent of the blood of this just person: see ye to it.

25 Then answered all the people, and said, 'His blood be on us and on our children.'

26 Then released he Barabbas unto them: and when he had scourged Jesus, he delivered him to be crucified."

Matthew 27:3-5, *"Then Judas, which had betrayed him, when he saw that he was condemned, repented himself, and brought again the thirty pieces of silver to the chief priests and elders, Saying, I have sinned in that I have betrayed the innocent blood. And they said, "What is that to us? See thou to that." And he cast down the pieces of silver in the temple, and departed, and went and hanged himself."*

Isaiah's prophecy, that he made his grave with the wicked and with the rich in his death.

After Jesus' crucifixion, He was placed in a rich man's tomb. **Matthew 27:57-60,** *"When the evening was come, there came a rich man of Arimathaea, named Joseph, who also himself was Jesus' disciple.*

He went to Pilate, and begged the body of Jesus. Then Pilate commanded the body to be delivered.

And when Joseph had taken the body, he wrapped it in a clean linen cloth, And laid it in his own new tomb, which he had hewn out in the rock: and he rolled a great stone to the door of the sepulcher, and departed."*

On two occasions, the Bible mentions Jesus cried out to His Father. He prayed in the Garden of Gethsemane and asked, *"Father, let this cup pass from me nevertheless not my will but thane be done."* Jesus knew His hour had come and understood the agony of the cross He would bear for the world's sins. So, now, in His humanistic nature, Jesus cried out.

Why did Jesus Cry Out On the Cross?

"My God, My God, why hast thou forsaken me?" Jesus is both human and God. As explained earlier, God is a spirit who indwells the human flesh of Jesus. He is the spirit of the very God and Creator. God put on flesh and came in the form of a man (represented by Jesus Christ), who sacrificed His life for the sins of the world. Consequently, Jesus could feel pain just as we do. When He prayed in the garden, His sweat became as if it were drops of blood. He knew the hour had come to face death. When he thought of the

agony of the cross, He asked, *"Father, if it be possible, let this cup pass from me."*

The body without the spirit is dead, so when Jesus cried out on the cross and then gave up the ghost, in that moment the Spirit of God left His body.

John 17:1-6, *"These words spake Jesus, and lifted up his eyes to heaven, and said, Father, the hour is come; glorify thy Son, that thy Son also may glorify thee:*

2 As thou hast given him power over all flesh, that he should give eternal life to as many as thou hast given him.

3 And this is life eternal, that they might know thee the only true God, and Jesus Christ, whom thou hast sent.

4 I have glorified thee on the earth: I have finished the work which thou gavest me to do.

5 And now, O Father, glorify thou me with thine own self with the glory which I had with thee before the world was.

6 I have manifested thy name unto the men which thou gavest me out of the world: thine they were, and thou gavest them me, and they have kept thy word."

Philippians 2:8 *"And being found in fashion as a man, he humbled himself and became obedient unto death, even the death of the cross."* For our sins and iniquities, Jesus was crucified, the Lamb slain from the foundation of the world.

A similar question was asked in **Isaiah 40:18 and 21-23.** *"To whom then will ye liken God? or What likeness will ye compare unto him?*

Have ye not known? have ye not heard? hath it not been told you from the beginning?

 Have ye not understood from the foundations of the earth?

 It is he that sitteth upon the circle of the earth, and the inhabitants thereof are as grasshoppers; that stretcheth out the heavens as a curtain, and spreadeth them out as a tent to dwell in: That bringeth the princes to nothing; he maketh the judges of the earth as vanity."

***Isaiah 40:25**, "To whom then will ye liken me, or shall I be equal? saith the Holy One (Jesus)."*

He went back to Heaven, but one day no one knows the day or the hour. He will return to take his chosen people to be with Him eternally. Will you be ready when he comes? Will you be ready to receive him as the King of Kings and Lord of Lords, your redeemer the only living God?

www.ingramcontent.com/pod-product-compliance
Lightning Source LLC
Chambersburg PA
CBHW071222160426
43196CB00012B/2387